LEENDERT JAN VIS

FOR YOU

FRONT STREET
ASHEVILLE, NORTH CAROLINA

IN THE TIME BEFORE I KNEW YOU...

Life was NOT a bed of roses.

IT was more like an endless,
rainy Sunday afternoon.

MOST OF THE TIME,
I PRACTICED
CLIMBING THE WALLS.

THINGS LOOKED
PRETTY NORMAL
ON THE OUTSIDE...

BUT I SENSED **SOMETHING** WAS MISSING.

One look and I knew...
I will never forget your face.

YOU ... YOU MAKE MY HEART SING.

BOOM! BADA BOOM! BOOM! BOO

WITH YOU I FEEL alive again!

I WANT TO DANCE WITH YOU.

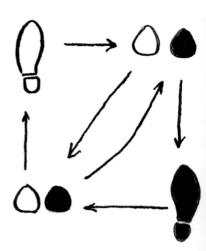

I WANT TO LAUGH WITH YOU.

HAHA HEE HEE HAHA HAHAHA

GREAT JOKE!

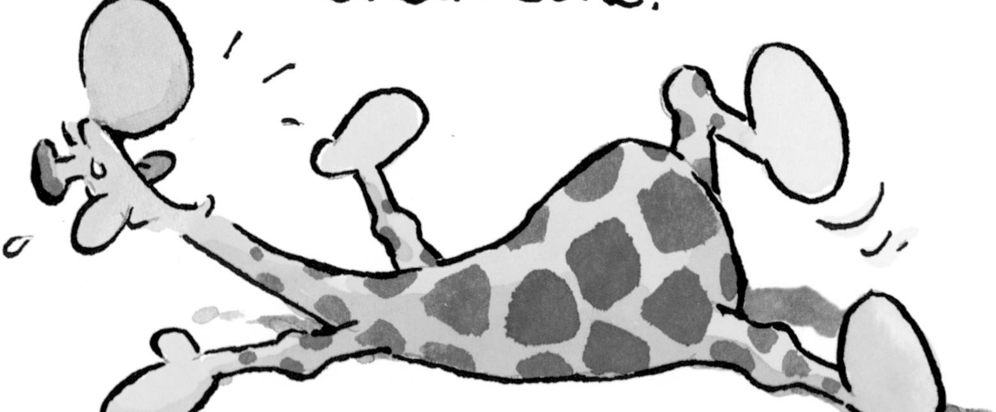

I WANT TO TALK WITH YOU FOR HOURS.

I WANT TO RUN BAREFOOT IN THE SAND WITH YOU.

I WANT TO CRAWL UNDER THE BLANKETS WITH YOU.

I WANT TO WAKE UP NEXT TO YOU.

I WANT TO GIVE YOU THE WORLD.

IT WOULD BE VERY NICE
if YOU
WANTED ME
TOO.

HOW aBOUT We GO RiGHT TO HaPPiLY eVer aFTer?